MEGA PLANTS

Written by Steve Pa

D1612872

CONTENTS

Collins

GIANTS OF THE FOREST

Forests are full of giants! They aren't pretend giants, like huge humans. They're real giants – trees. These mega plants are the tallest, widest and heaviest living things on Earth.

As well as giant trees in the forest, there are also mega plant parts. These include massive **leaves**, enormous **flowers**, extra-deep **roots** and super-sized **seeds**.

Many animals use mega plants for food. Tiny bugs suck their juices. Birds peck their seeds. Deer chew their leaves.

HOW TREES WORK

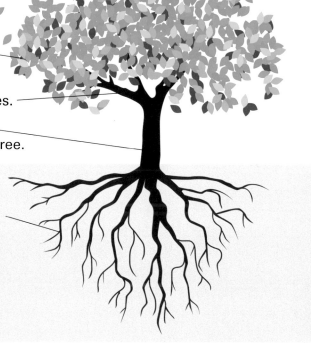

Leaves capture light energy from the sun.

Branches hold out leaves.

A woody **stem** called the **trunk** holds up the tree.

Roots take in water and **nutrients** from soil.

All plants live and grow using light energy from the Sun, and water and nutrients from the soil. Animals are different. They live and grow by eating food.

Conifer cones contain the tree's seeds.

The biggest trees are **conifers**. Most have thin, sharp leaves, but no flowers. Their seeds grow in **cones**.

BIGGEST OF ALL

One way to measure the biggest is by weight. The heaviest mega plants are giant redwood trees, also called giant sequoias. Greatest of all is a giant redwood called General Sherman. It lives in a forest in California, USA. It weighs over 2,000 tonnes. That's more than 50 enormous trucks, ten blue whales or 200 elephants!

Most of a tree's weight is its trunk. This is its stem – the part of the plant that holds up the branches, leaves and other parts. Trees have stems strengthened with tough, stringy fibres we call **wood**.

General Sherman isn't only very heavy. It's also extremely old, at more than 2,000 years of age.

4

The largest trees are much more massive than the biggest animals – elephants on land, and blue whales in the sea.

elephant
height four metres
weight ten tonnes

Dreadnoughtus dinosaur
length 26 metres
weight 50 tonnes

blue whale
length 30 metres
weight 200 tonnes

giant redwood
height 84 metres
weight over 2,000 tonnes

5

TALLEST AND WIDEST

Mega plants include those that are very tall or very wide. The tallest trees are coast redwoods, found in north-west North America. Some are over 100 metres high.

Other super-tall trees are coastal Douglas firs, also in North America, and the mountain ash, a kind of gumtree (eucalyptus) that lives in North America.

A few of the coastal redwoods in California, USA, grow to more than 110 metres tall.

The widest trees include baobabs, mostly in Africa. It would take more than 20 people, holding hands, to go all around the trunk of one baobab. Giant redwoods and coast redwoods are also very wide.

The Sunland baobab tree in South Africa is so wide that you can sit inside and buy a drink!

EVEN MORE MEGA!

Another way to be a mega plant is to have the most branches that spread the farthest. In India, some banyan trees have branches that cover an area of two football pitches!

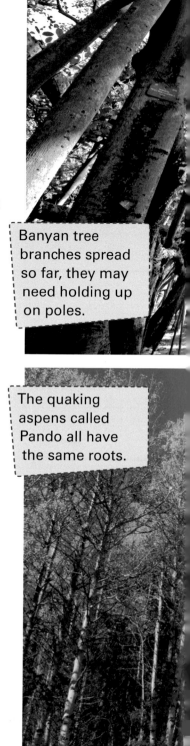

Banyan tree branches spread so far, they may need holding up on poles.

Some trees live so close together that they could be one mega plant. In Utah, in south-west United States, thousands of trees called quaking aspens all grow next to each other. Each has its own trunk and branches. But under the ground, all the trees grow from one enormous set of roots. Some experts say it's many trees. Others say it's one tree, called Pando.

The quaking aspens called Pando all have the same roots.

The quaking aspens of Pando all share the same roots. These are the plant parts that take in water and nutrients from the soil, and also hold the plant firmly so it doesn't topple over.

8

9

HUGE LEAVES AND SEEDS

As well as mega plants, there are mega plant parts.
These include leaves, seeds, flowers and roots.

The largest single leaves belong to the giant water lily.
They are like round, flat tables floating on the water.
Some of these leaves are bigger than a real table, at more
than two metres across.

Giant waterlilies grow in the Amazon
River, South America. They float so
well, a child could sit on one.

Palms have long, stringy leaves, and long, stringy flowers too!

The royal raphia palm is the tree that gives us the string-like fibres called raffia. Each leaf can be 25 metres long, but it has lots of small strips rather than one wide surface.

The biggest seeds are from the coco-de-mer palm tree. Each seed looks like two coconuts joined together, and is more than 30 centimetres across.

Coco-de-mer palm trees are found on islands in the Indian Ocean. Each seed weighs 20 kilograms.

SUPER FLOWERS

Flowers are the parts of a plant that make seeds. The seeds have tiny baby plants inside. They are spread by animals, wind or water. When they reach a suitable place with damp soil, they start growing into new plants.

Imagine a flower on a table, which is as big as the table! The world's most mega flower is the rafflesia. It grows in the gloomy rainforests of South East Asia.

The rafflesia flower is up to one metre across. It opens out from a **bud**, makes its smell and shrivels away, all in just a few days.

The rafflesia smells like horrible rotten flesh. This helps it to breed or reproduce. The stink attracts flies and other bugs to the flower, which pick up its tiny **pollen** grains. The bugs then carry the pollen to other rafflesias, so they can make seeds.

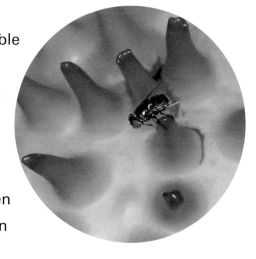

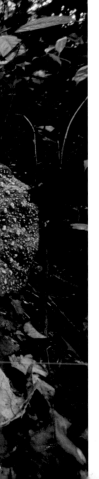

The titan arum can grow over three metres tall, but it's really a collection of smaller flowers rather than a single one.

13

FASTEST AND DEEPEST

Mega plant parts include roots in the soil. These take in water and nutrients, which flow along tiny tubes to the plant's stem, and up the stem to the leaves and flowers.

Plants in deserts and dry places have extra-long roots to search for water. In southern Africa, wild fig trees have roots that go down 90 metres. In North America, tree-sized cactus plants have roots that spread out 50 metres.

The roots of a wild fig tree go down as deep as a football pitch is long!

14

In one day, a bamboo grows taller by the length of your arm!

There are mega plant growers too. Fastest growing are bamboos, which are kinds of giant grass with stiff, woody stems. In their warm, damp forest homes in China, they can grow by 80 centimetres or more every day!

WEIRD MONSTERS

Some plants are not only hugely mega, they are very strange too.

The weirdest leaves belong to the welwitschia of southern Africa. All through its life, it has only two leaves. Each grows more than five metres long, gets tangled around itself, and is torn by wind and nibbled by animals.

Welwitschia leaves are as old as the whole plant, which could be 1,000 years.

Pitcher plants catch and rot away, or digest, small animals for extra food.

The nastiest creature-eater plant is Attenborough's pitcher of the Philippines, East Asia. Bugs and other small animals, like mice and lizards, fall into the vase-shaped pitcher. Here they drown and rot away in the strong juices.

The fiercest thorns grow on the honey locust tree from North America. The thorns grow in groups and are more than 20 centimetres in length.

The thorns of the honey locust tree get harder as they grow older.

GIANTS OF THE SEA

There are no huge trees or enormous flowers in the sea. But around the shores are mega plants called seaweeds. The biggest is giant kelp, found along the shores of the Pacific Ocean. It grows to more than 40 metres long, and waves to and fro in the water.

In underwater forests of giant kelp, creatures such as fish, seals and sea otters hide and feed.

Seagrass is tasty food for animals such as manatees, green turtles, crabs and urchins.

A few kinds of grass grow in the sea. They're called seagrass! Their leaves reach one metre in length and swish to and fro in the water, like long grass blowing in the wind on land.

To grow and stay healthy, seagrass has the same three main needs as all plants.

1 light

2 water

3 nutrients

Seagrass only grows in shallow water. It's too dark in deep water.

Seagrass has water all around!

Seagrass roots take up nutrients from the seabed mud.

BIGGEST YET SMALLEST?

In the middle of the sea, there are no trees or flowers, and very few seaweeds. Yet there are plenty of fish, seals, whales and other animals. Where does their food come from?

The answer is too small to see. Floating in the oceans are millions and billions of tiny plant-like living things, called plant plankton. All added together, they would weigh as much as all the farm plants we grow on land, all around the world!

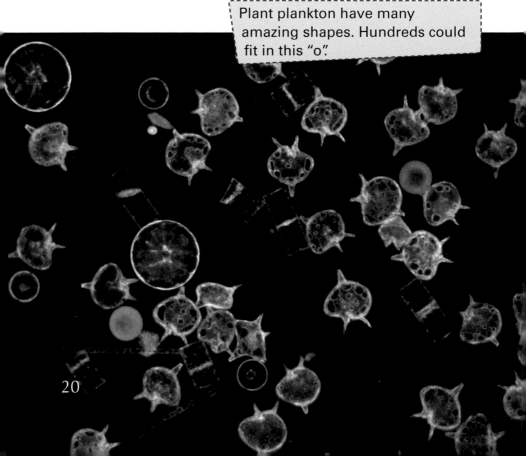

Plant plankton have many amazing shapes. Hundreds could fit in this "o".

FOOD CHAIN

Plant plankton are eaten by little creatures like fish and shrimps. These get eaten by bigger creatures, and so on, to the biggest sharks and whales.

plant plankton

krill

whale shark

Lists of who eats what are called food chains. All ocean food chains begin with plant plankton.

HOW MEGA PLANTS BEGAN

Long ago, there were no plants on land, and only little plants in the sea. Gradually, small plants began to grow along the shore. Slowly, new kinds spread over the land. Over millions of years, they became bigger – the first mega plants.

The first really tall plants were wattiezas, about ten metres high. They lived almost 400 million years ago and looked similar to tree ferns today.

In the mega forests of 300 million years ago lived giant dragonflies as big as crows.

22

By 300 million years ago, the biggest forests the world has ever seen covered half of all the land.

Why were forests so huge millions of years ago, compared to today? It was warm and damp all around the world then, which helped plants to grow faster and in more places. Also, there were fewer animals to eat them, and no people to chop them down!

MONSTERS OF THE PAST – AND FUTURE?

Mega plants of the past left **fossils**. The biggest fossil is part of a tualang tree trunk 72 metres long. It shows that when the tree was alive, almost one million years ago, it was over 100 metres high.

The biggest ever fossil trunk was from a tualang tree and was found in Thailand.

Ginkgoes in today's parks have good soil and aren't crowded by other trees. This may be why they grow bigger than long ago.

Ginkgo trees have been around since the age of dinosaurs, more than 200 million years ago. Yet ginkgoes today are growing taller than they did long ago. Some are massive, more than 60 metres high. In the future, could they get even more mega?

MOST MEGA OF ALL

Giant trees and other mega plants are huge. But are
they the biggest of all living things? Even larger could
be fungi – what we usually call mushrooms, toadstools
and moulds. The mushroom or toadstool is only
a tiny part. Most of the **fungus** lives underneath in the soil,
as a tangle of threads and fibres that spreads widely
all around.

In Oregon, USA, lives the most mega mould of all –
the Humongous Fungus. It's a honey fungus whose soil
threads cover an area of 100 football pitches. It weighs up
to 1,000 tonnes.

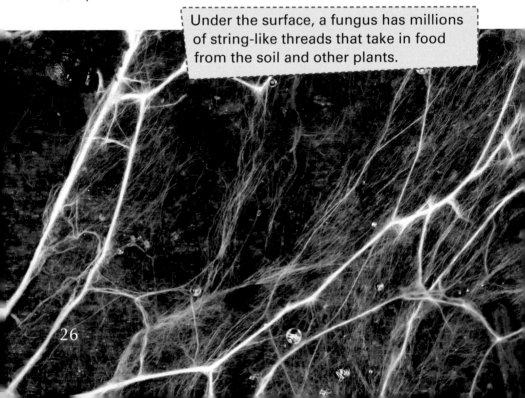

Under the surface, a fungus has millions
of string-like threads that take in food
from the soil and other plants.

Maybe even bigger fungi wait to be discovered, perhaps in a wood near you!

The only part of a honey fungus above the soil is the mushroom.

GLOSSARY

branches parts of a tree that spread out from the main trunk, to hold out the leaves, flowers and seeds

bud a small, rounded plant part, from which the flower opens out

cones hard, woody parts of conifer trees that contain the seeds

conifers trees that have woody cones to make their seeds, rather than flowers

flowers the parts of a plant that make seeds; many flowers have bright, colourful parts called petals

fossils remains of living things that have died, are buried, and are preserved in the rocks

fungus a kind of living thing that gets its food from rotting plants and animals

leaves plant parts that take in or capture light energy from the sun, which they use to live and grow

nutrients substances that living things use to live and grow, also called food or nourishment

pollen tiny grains, that look like dust or sand, that help a flower make its seeds

roots underground plant parts that take in water and nutrients

seeds small, tough parts that grow into new plants

stem the part of a plant above the ground, which holds up the leaves and flowers

trunk the main tall woody part or stem of a tree, that holds up the branches

wood strong, tough fibres or threads that strengthen the stem of a tree, bush or shrub

INDEX

MEGA PLANTS AROUND THE WORLD

Pando quaking aspens

Humongous Fungus

coastal redwoods

giant kelp

General Sherman
giant redwood

giant waterlilies

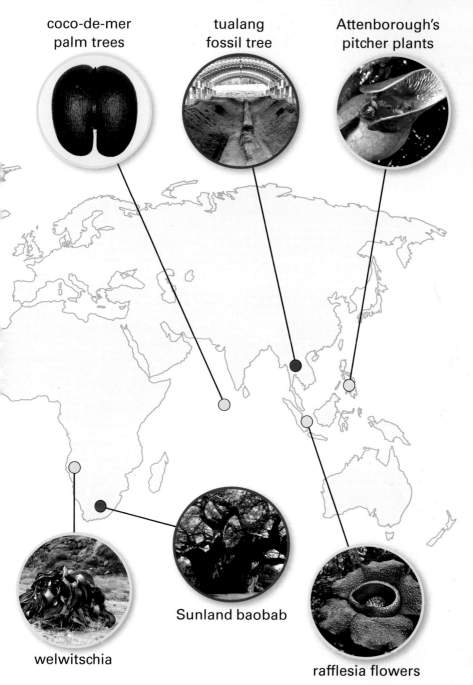

coco-de-mer palm trees

tualang fossil tree

Attenborough's pitcher plants

welwitschia

Sunland baobab

rafflesia flowers

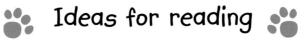

Ideas for reading

Written by Clare Dowdall, PhD
Lecturer and Primary Literacy Consultant

Reading objectives:
- retrieve and record information from non-fiction
- use dictionaries to check the meaning of words
- ask questions to improve understanding
- identify how language, structure and presentation contribute to meaning

Spoken language objectives:
- ask relevant questions to extend their understanding and knowledge

Curriculum links:
Science: plants; Geography: locational knowledge

Resources: mirrors, pencils and papers, tape measures, digital cameras, junk materials

Build a context for reading
- Ask children to talk about any strange or amazing plants that they have ever seen. Ask about cacti, toadstools, etc.
- Challenge children to describe what they can see on the front cover. Support them to use a range of adjectives to describe the trunk to build their vocabulary.
- Read the title and blurb together. Discuss what "mega" means. Challenge children to suggest other words that have "mega" as a prefix. Model how to look up the meaning in a dictionary and make connections to the theme of plants.

Understand and apply reading strategies
- Look at the contents. Discuss how the information is organised to interest the reader.
- Read the chapter headings *Giants of the forest* and *Weird monsters*. Ask children to suggest what these chapter headings mean.
- Turn to pp2–3. Ask children to read the content quietly to themselves. Challenge children to read closely to find answers to simple questions about the content, e.g. *How do trees work? How are plants and animals different?*